D1202849

Village to Village Traveling Quilt
Freedom Seekers from Jackson, Michigan's Past & Present

Diane Washington
Illustrated by Jerome Washington

Season Press
Kalamazoo, Michigan

Bringing the village to life

This book celebrates the bravery and resilience of African American pioneers and freedom seekers who came to Jackson, Michigan in the 19th century. These historical figures played an important role in the city's growth and development.

From the villages of Africa to the villages in America, all of us are bound in a single human tapestry like the patches in a multicolored quilt. The common thread binding all the pages of this book is a sense of connection that joins the past to the present, youth to seniors, and families to the community.

Diane Washington

Emma Nichols

Emma Nichols was a freedom seeker who escaped from a Virginia plantation in the 1850s with help from the Underground Railroad. She came to Jackson, where she worked as a seamstress. Many of the designs in the Underground Railroad quilt symbolize the challenges that freedom seekers like Emma faced on their journey north.

Wagon Wheel

Debra Guinn

Present-day seamstress Debra Guinn of Jackson helped create an intergenerational quilt program with Young People of Purpose (YPOP) . The designs in the Underground Railroad quilt symbolize the challenges that freedom seekers faced on their journey.

Underground Railroad Map

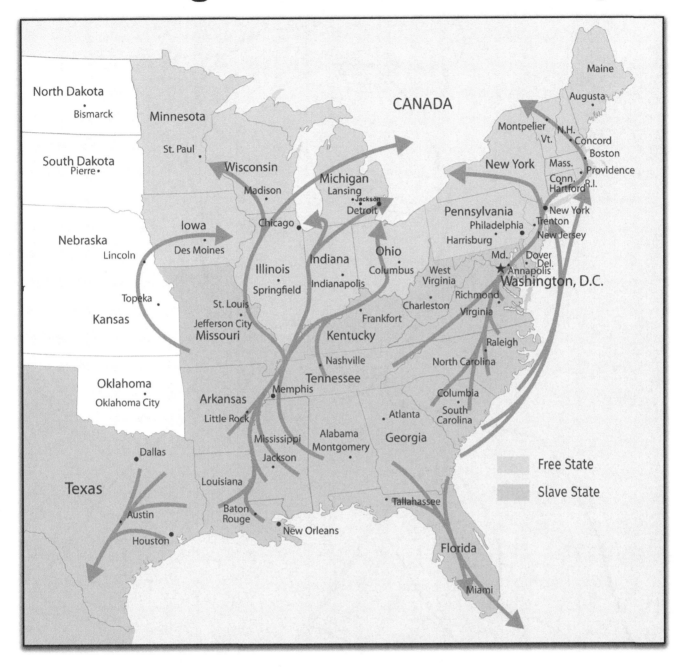

The Underground Railroad was a secret system for freedom seekers and abolitionists who collaborated in the resistance to slavery. Different forms of transportation were used to move enslaved people in the South to free states in the North and other countries. They often conducted travel at night and hiding places included homes, barns, and cellars.

This quilt pattern by present-day seamstress Nmesoma Journey shows how the enslaved sometimes chose different pathways on the Underground Railroad to escape to safety.

Color your Log Cabin quilt pattern

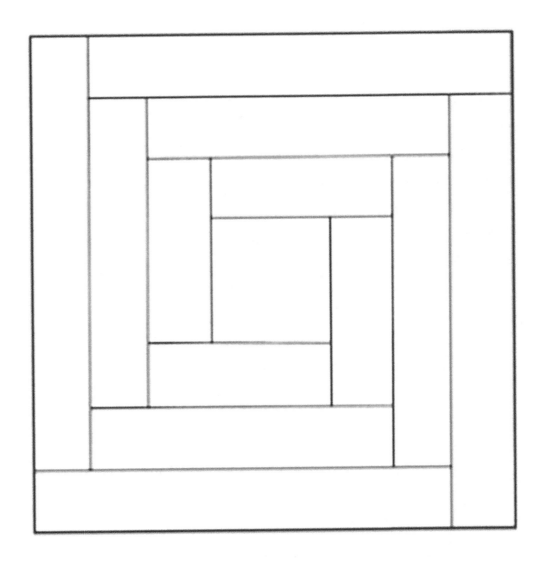

The distance from Virginia to Michigan is more than 470 miles. Passengers on the underground railroad may have taken shelter and protection in the home of supporters along the way. This Log Cabin pattern of a quilt square represents the Underground Railroad quilt.

George Brown
Mason

George Brown
showed great strength
and endurance as he built
Jackson's Stonewall in the
1860s. Today, Stonewall
Road is named for the
wall located near
Ella Sharp Park.

The Crazy Quilt pattern was sewn by YPOP student Ah'zjawnah Smith for the Underground Railroad African American Quilt project in Jackson.

Freedom seekers may have looked to the North Star for direction to freedom. The never-moving North Star, represented in this quilt pattern, helped guide freedom seekers northward.

You can find the North Star by first finding the Big Dipper. Then plot a straight line upward from the outer rim of the cup.

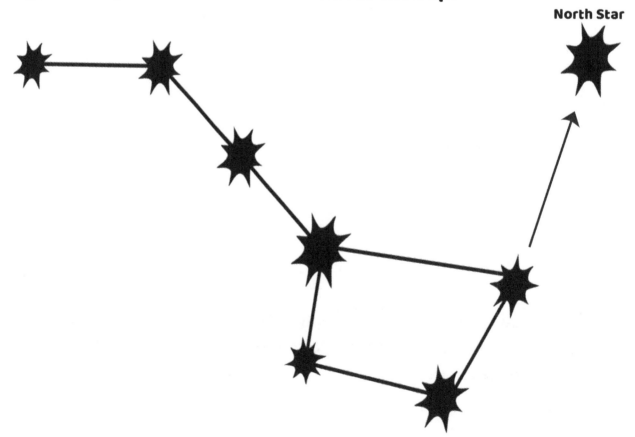

North Star

Color your harvest

YPOP Garden Vegetables & Fruit

Freedom seekers who traveled during the summer may have picked vegetables and fruit for food along the way. The YPOP students distributed produce grown in the Village Gardens to the community of Jackson to help with food insecurity.

Lena Reynolds
Gardner

Lena Reynolds traveled from her home in the south to live in Jackson. She is an important part of the YPOP Village Gardens.

Taylor Carter
Firefighter

Taylor Carter was a firefighter in the 1880s. He was the first African American firefighter in Jackson.

Thomas Tryst
Pioneer

Thomas Tryst (also spelled Trist) came to Jackson in 1835. He was the first African American in the city and worked as a blacksmith.

Richard Nichols
Barber

Richard Nichols escaped from a Virginia plantation in the 1850s. He came to Jackson on the Underground Railroad and later owned a barbershop in the city.

Emma Patton-Nichols
Seamstress

Emma Patton-Nichols escaped a Virginia plantation in the 1850s. She came to Jackson on the Underground Railroad and worked as a seamstress. She was the wife of Richard Nichols.

George Green
Church Co-Founder

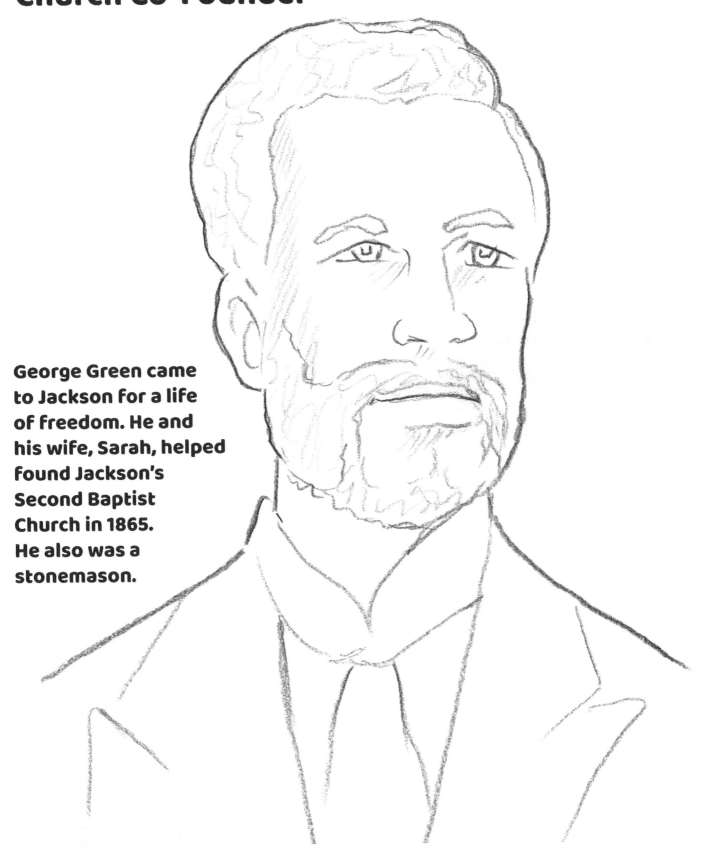

George Green came to Jackson for a life of freedom. He and his wife, Sarah, helped found Jackson's Second Baptist Church in 1865. He also was a stonemason.

Sarah Green
Church Co-Founder

Sarah Green escaped to freedom in the north and came to Jackson. She and her husband, George, helped found Second Baptist Church in Jackson, where she served as a leader.

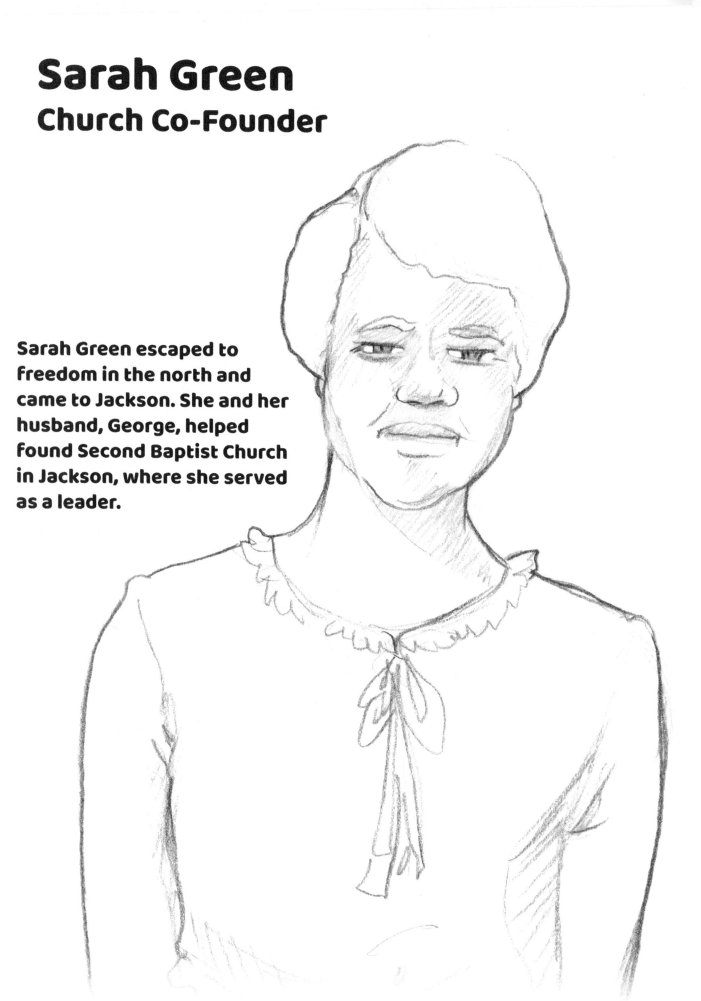

Rev. Polk Williams
Pastor

The Rev. Polk Williams served as the pastor of Second Baptist Church. He was a community leader and one of the longest-serving pastors in Jackson.

Darius Williams
Pastor

**Darius Williams is the pastor of Second Missionary Baptist Church*.
He also is a Jackson County Commissioner. His wife, Mia, is an attorney.**

*Darius Williams is the pastor at the date of this publication in 2022.

Frank Thurman
Coroner & Politician

Frank Thurman was a coroner in Jackson and in 1880 became the city's first African American elected official.

Lucy Thurman
Activist

Lucy Thurman was the co-founder of Women's Christian Temperance Union. She served as National Superintendent of Work Among Colored People. She was the wife of Frank Thurman.

Jacob Hamilton
Solider

Jacob Hamilton was a soldier in the 102nd Regiment, U.S. Colored Infantry, Company B. His troop served in the Civil War from 1863 to 1865.

Sarah Hamilton
Dressmaker

Sarah Hamilton was the wife of Jacob Hamilton. She worked as a dressmaker in Jackson.

Gurtie Crater
Seamstress

Gertie Crater is a seamstress and served as senior advisor of the YPOP Intergenerational African American Underground Railroad Quilt project.

Diane Washington
Youth Leader & Entrepreneur

Diane Washington founded Young People of Purpose (YPOP). She also is an entrepreneur and author of the book, Annie's Amazing Art Venture and Village to Village Traveling Quilt.

Match the history makers with their picture

1. Emma Nichols

2. Richard Nichols

3. Sarah Green

4. George Green

5. Lucy Thurman

6. Frank Thurman

7. Jacob Hamilton

8. Sarah Hamilton

Word scramble
Unscramble these words

1. ddnrnrogueu dlraoair

2. yvalser

3. pcsaee

4. htorn rsta

5. treecs

6. mdfroee

7. tuliq

8. ryhisot

Draw Your Own Beautiful Quilt

Use this space to draw your own quilt. Make your own memories and pick your own beautiful colors!

What does freedom mean to you?

The Underground Railroad was dedicated to helping people achieve freedom. Write what freedom means to you.

_____

_____

_____

_____

_____

_____

_____

Help Clara find her way along the Underground Railroad from her Village in Shakaanda, South Africa, to Carson Village in Jackson. She wants to meet her friend Annie.

*Start at the bottom so Clara can meet freedom seekers along the way.

South Africa

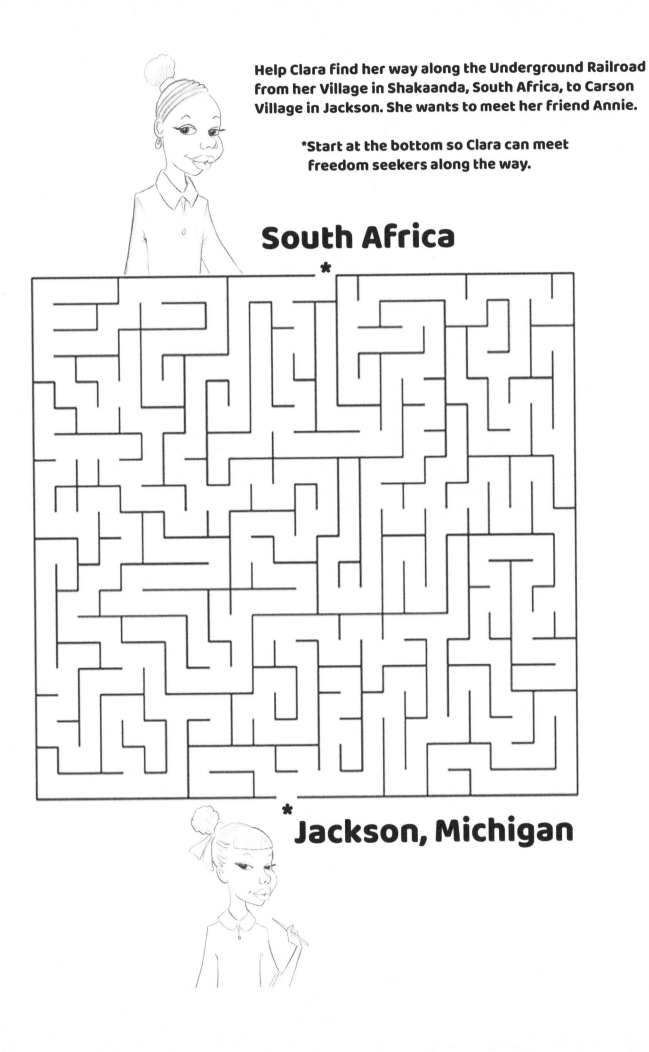

* Jackson, Michigan

ANSWERS

Match the history makers with their picture
Answers

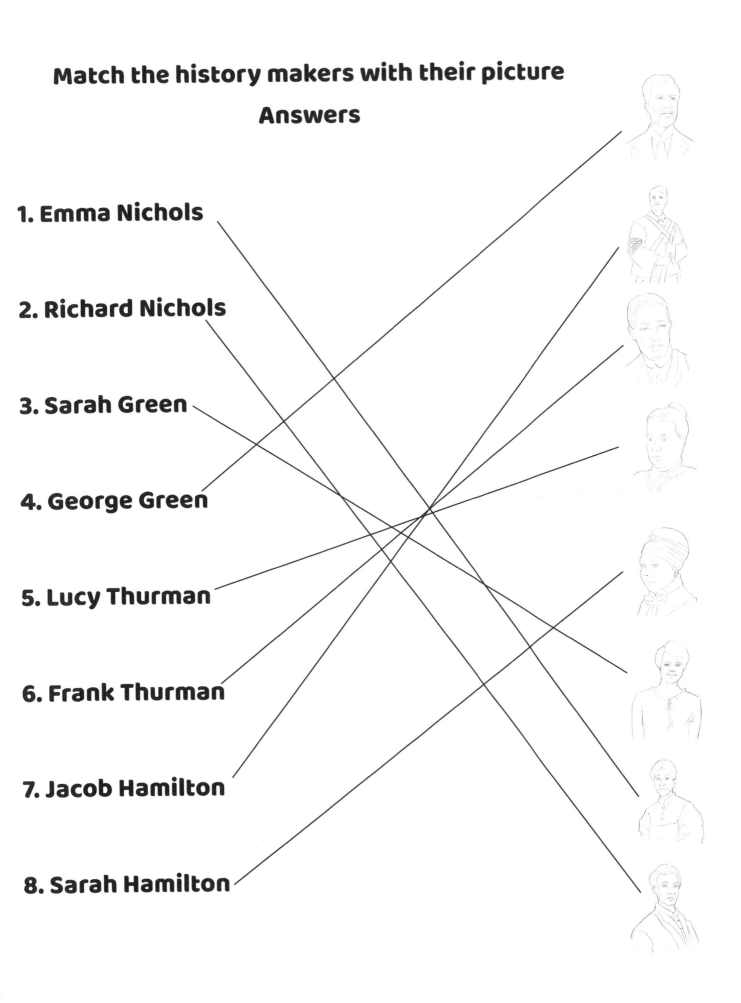

1. Emma Nichols

2. Richard Nichols

3. Sarah Green

4. George Green

5. Lucy Thurman

6. Frank Thurman

7. Jacob Hamilton

8. Sarah Hamilton

Word scramble Answers

1. Underground Railroad

2. Slavery

3. Escape

4. North Star

5. Secret

6. Freedom

7. Quilt

8. History

19th Century African Americans in Jackson
(in chronological order)

1835 - Thomas Tryst (also spelled "Trist") established a blacksmith shop west of Jackson Street. Thomas was the first African American in the City of Jackson.

1850s - Emma Nichols came to Jackson after escaping from a plantation in Virginia and traveled North, with help from the Underground Railroad. In Jackson, she married Richard Nichols and worked as a seamstress. The couple raised a family, which included daughter, Carrie Nichols Bowles.

1850s - Richard Nichols came to Jackson after escaping from a plantation in Virginia and traveled North, with help from the Underground Railroad. In Jackson, he worked as a barber. He and his wife Emma Nichols are buried in Mt. Evergreen Cemetery, Jackson.

1860s - George Brown built a stone wall on the southwest side of the Merriman farm near the Ella Sharp Park. George was a stonemason from New York. His handiwork, which is cut so precisely it still stands, is the namesake of "Stonewall Road."

1863-65 – Jacob Hamilton, a Civil War freedom fighter who served in the 102nd Regiment, U.S. Colored Infantry, (originally the 1st Michigan Colored Regiment) from 1863-5. He lived in Jackson in his later years and is buried in the Soldier's Field section of Mt. Evergreen Cemetery.

1865 - George Green co-founded the Second Baptist Church (today the Second Missionary Baptist Church) with his wife Sarah in their home on Pearl Street. George was a former enslaved American who came to Jackson from Virginia after the Civil War. He was a stonemason by trade and helped build the original church. Today, the congregation represents one of Jackson's sesquicentennial churches.

1865 - Sarah Green co-founded the Second Baptist Church (today the Second Missionary Baptist Church) with her husband George in their home on Pearl Street. Sarah was a former enslaved American who came to Jackson from Virginia after the Civil War. She led a women's group that helped to build the church. Today, the congregation represents one of Jackson's sesquicentennial churches.

1880 – Sarah Hamilton worked as a dressmaker in downtown Jackson. She was the wife of Civil War soldier Jacob Hamilton.

1880 – Frank Thurman was elected to the position of "coroner." He was the first black person to hold an elected county position. He was the husband of Lucy Thurman.

1880s - Taylor Carter served as Jackson's first black firefighter.

1890s - Lucinda "Lucy" Thurman co-founded the Women's Christian Temperance Union (WCTU) and the National Superintendent of Work Among Colored People under the WCTUs. Lucy lectured around the nation and in Great Britain. Lucy, who is a Michigan Hall of Fame honoree, was married to Frank Thurman.

* Some drawings have been drawn to resemble a likeness or an image appropriate to the time period of these freedom seekers if no photos were available.

Explore Jackson

There are several sites in Jackson that can help you understand Emma's journey to freedom on the Underground Railroad. Below are a few possibilities:

Jackson, Michigan's Underground Railroad Historical Marker
This cast iron state marker honors the final resting place of local Underground Railroad participants, including Emma and Richard Nichols. It is located in Mt. Evergreen Cemetery near the intersection of Morrell Street and Greenwood Avenue.

Emma Nichols Garden
This walking path, with a plaque in Emma's honor, is surrounded by murals and is enlivened by landscaping. The path connects West Michigan Ave., to a parking lot behind City Hall in downtown Jackson.

Self-guided Underground Railroad Walking Tour
This website is offered by Experience Jackson, the Jackson County Visitors Bureau. It enables visitors to download a self-guided walking tour of historic sites in and around downtown Jackson. For more, see: www.experiencejackson.com/app

The YPOP Garden
Among the plants in this garden are tomatoes, peppers cabbage, corn—vegetables that Emma could have eaten along her journey if she escaped in summer. The YPOP Village Community and Educational Gardens, created by Diane Washington of YPOP EXPLORERS, Young People of Purpose, are dedicated to building a strong village and a hopeful future. Visit the Gardens located at 1107 and 1102 Maple Ave.

For more information on Jackson's role in the Underground Railroad, including the Nichols, local activists who helped them, and related reading material see:

Jacksonmiundergroundrailroad.com

About the Traveling Quilt Project Creators

About the Author

Diane Washington is an entrepreneur, businesswoman, and community leader who has worked with schools and community organizations across the state. She is the Founder and Executive Director of YPOP EXPLORERS, Young People of Purpose, a non-profit organization that empowers youth to learn and serve.

This Village to Village Traveling Quilt Coloring Book follows Diane's first publication, Annie's Amazing Art Venture, which promotes hands-on exploration and learning opportunities for youth and the community. Diane's projects reflect her many skills, including painting, storytelling, and her experiences as a Master Gardener and world traveler. Diane is committed to leading and serving others with zest and fervor, by the grace of God. She and her husband Pastor Starlon Washington, have 6 children.

About the Illustrator

Jerome Washington, (Diane's brother-in-law) created the illustrations for this book, as well as Diane's other book, Annie's Amazing Art Venture. Jerome is well-known throughout West Michigan for his caricatures of students and community leaders. He has illustrated several commissioned works and his creations have been featured in the Battle Creek Art Center in Battle Creek, MI, as well as several businesses, schools, and government offices in Albion and throughout Michigan.

About the Historical Consultant

Linda Hass is a historical researcher/writer/presenter with a special interest in the Underground Railroad. She has written three books on the subject and has successfully applied for several state and national historical designations involving Jackson.

Thank you to all who helped bring this village and book to life. A special thank you to Linda Hass for her great research and consultation and to the Ella Sharp Museum for their Bringing the Village to Life exhibit.

Diane Washington
P.O. Box 1206
Jackson, MI 49204
www.youngpeopleofpurpose.org

Published in collaboration with Fortitude Graphic Design & Printing and Season Press LLC.
Illustrated by Jerome Washington
Design and layout by Sean Hollins

Printed in the United States of America

Publisher's Cataloging-in-Publication data
Washington, Diane
Village to Village Traveling Quilt: Freedom Seekers from
Jackson, Michigan's Past & Present / Diane Washington
p. cm.

ISBN 978-1-7370202-7-1
1. Jackson, Michigan—History —African American
2. Underground Railroad
3. Quilts-African American History

First Edition
10 9 8 7 6 5 4 3 2 1

Made in the USA
Middletown, DE
20 February 2022

61585791R00024